CELEBRATIN

*C*HRISTMAS
Book 2

DONALD HILTON

FESTIVAL SERVICES for the Church Year

Other books by Donald Hilton

Boy into Man
Girl into Woman
Celebrating Series
Six Men and a Pulpit
Risks of Faith
Raw Materials of Faith
Results of Faith
After Much Discussion

Compiled by Donald Hilton

A Word in Season
Prayers for the Church Community
(with Roy Chapman)

Published by:
National Christian Education Council
Robert Denholm House
Nutfield
Redhill RH1 4HW

British Library Cataloguing-in-Publication Data;
Hilton, Donald 1932-
Celebrating Christmas – 2nd ed.
Bk.2
1. Christian church. Public worship – Rites
I. Title II. National Christian Education Council
264

ISBN 0-7197-0451-0

Typeset by One and a Half Graphics, Redhill, Surrey
Printed by Halstan & Co Ltd, Amersham, Buckinghamshire

PREFACE

This book contains four Festival Services involving all ages in the church and designed for use in the period before Christmas, or on Christmas Day itself. Minor alterations of language may be necessary according to the proximity of Christmas.

The services began their life in a local church and have been written up for wider circulation. They will be found most useful where the leader of the service meets with those who work with the various age groups and adapts the scripts to meet local needs and opportunities.

An important assumption behind these services is that in the celebration of the Christian Festivals every age group has something to contribute. Festival Services are not events planned so that children can entertain adults. They are celebrations by the whole church family, for the whole church family.

No place is given in the orders of service for either the Lord's Prayer or an offertory. These can be inserted according to local custom.

CONTENTS

SOUNDS LIKE CHRISTMAS

Introduction
This service exploits the fact that Christmas has its own distinctive sounds. We remind ourselves of some of them, hear others, and use the sounds to deepen our awareness of the meaning of Christmas.

Preparation
Each of the sounds to be used needs to be prepared carefully:

Carol singers Arrange for a mixed age group of carol singers to be in the church porch, or in the street outside the church, as people arrive. Position them so that they can also be heard from inside the church.

Christmas music Obtain a cassette of Christmas music. It need not be religious music. A pop group's Christmas song will serve the purpose well.

Bells Tape-record local bells or obtain a record/cassette of bells pealing joyfully.

Party sounds Have ready a number of crackers, party poppers, balloons etc. Poppers which project streamers are especially effective. Plan a simple singing game for the children to play with piano accompaniment. It will be important to create a sense of spontaneity despite the fact that it must be well prepared.

The cry of a baby Record, or obtain a recording of, a baby crying. Carefully rehearse the point where this is used to bring out the meaning of the reading it illustrates.

The Festival Service

Carols are sung by a group as people arrive at the church. They continue, heard by the congregation from a distance, up to and during the call to worship.

Call to worship
I will sing the story of thy love, O Lord, for ever;
I will proclaim thy faithfulness to all generations.
Thy true love is firm as the ancient earth,
thy faithfulness fixed as the heavens.
Blessed is the Lord for ever. (Psalm 89.1-2,52 NEB)

Invite the carol singers into church. Let them sing another carol alone, then invite the congregation to sing one with them. The singers then sit in the congregation.

Leader Few sounds evoke the feeling of Christmas more than the sound of carollers, their voices carrying over the night air. When we first hear them each year it really sounds like Christmas. And there are other sounds that tell us Christmas is here. A cheerful 'Happy Christmas' is one. *If the service is taking place very close to Christmas invite each member of the congregation to give Christmas greetings to the people sitting near to them.* In this service we will hear the sounds of Christmas and let them help us understand the meaning of this happy and special time of the year.

Reading The shepherds hear the song of glory: Luke 2.8-14

Prayer
> The heaven of heavens declares your glory, eternal God,
>> earth and sky combine to speak your praise,
>> north and south, east and west unite in songs of love,
>> from depth of earth to highest heaven: Glory to God!
> And now your favour rests on us,
>> the promised Christ has made his home on earth,
>> the long-awaited Lord is present with his people,
>> and his coming is for our blessing and hope.
> Let there be peace on earth,
>> peace in our hearts of men and women,
>> peace in our homes and relationships,
>> peace between nations;
>> the very peace of God.
> Glory to God in highest heaven, and on earth his peace
> for those on whom his favour rests.

As the prayer concludes play the record/cassette of joyful bells for several minutes.

Hymn Ding, dong! merrily on high

Story
The Sound of Christmas Mail
This story comes from Norway, a land of deep snow and freezing winter temperatures. It happened long before the days of mail vans and tractors. The mail was delivered by foot or on horses, and in Norway sometimes on skis or a sledge. Rat-a-tat-tat was the sound people liked to hear. They knew the postmen had put a letter through their door, or maybe was standing there with a parcel in his hand.

Ola was a young teenager and he was proud of his father. His father was the postman and daily travelled around the many villages and farms that surrounded the small village where they lived.

Summer was fine. Father could cycle or walk with the letters he picked up from the railway station each morning to deliver to the people. But winter was different. Then he needed the help of Blackie, their plucky little horse. Sometimes the snow was too high even for Blackie. Then father had to put on his skis. Being the postman was a hard job, but Ola had long since decided that it was the one he wanted to do when he was old enough. He could imagine the rat-a-tat-tat on the door as excited people inside the houses came to see what post there was for them.

Tomorrow was the great day for the postman, the day when everyone expected letters and parcels. Tomorrow was Christmas Eve. Ola wished he could go with his father. He had often travelled with him in the summer so he knew the way; but never in the winter. But one day he would. He knew it! The people would rush to the door as they heard his Christmas rat-a-tat-tat.

Everything at home was ready for Christmas. The tree was cut from the forest, the house decorated, the sausages and hams were hanging from the roof, the smell of cakes and pastries came from the kitchen where his mother was working.

Ola was walking back from the barn where they kept their two cows during the winter months when his sister Marit came rushing across the snow-clad yard. 'Quickly! Come quickly!' she was shouting. 'Father has hurt himself. It's his leg. I'm sure it's broken. What shall we do?'

Inside the house his father was lying on a couch, mother watching over him as the doctor examined his leg. When the doctor sadly shook his head Ola knew that his sister was right.

'Well,' said his father as soon as the doctor had gone. 'Can you do it? You know the way well enough but can you do it in this weather? Or do we have to let the people down?'

Rat-a-tat-tat. The sound kept running through Ola's head; the Christmas sound that everyone would be expecting to hear tomorrow. He must do it! He simply must!

At four o'clock the next morning, Christmas Eve, his mother woke him. With hot porridge inside him and thick warm clothes on his back he was soon off into the countryside. It was pitch black but he knew the way to the railway station to pick up the post. And even if he hadn't known the way, Blackie could have got there blindfold.

'Good morning, Mr Olsen,' Ola called as he reached the station. The sky was clearer now and lights were appearing in the cottage windows. Ola explained about his father. 'You've got a hard job on if the snow keeps falling like this,' Mr Olsen said. 'But you are tough, like your father. Have a cup of coffee before you start.'

Off along the road they went. Ola rode astride Blackie who was pulling a great sledge piled with letters and parcels. To tell the truth, Ola felt a bit like Father Christmas! Rat-a-tat-tat. The sound echoed down the little streets as he knocked on the first door and handed two parcels and six letters to the old lady. All through the first village he went. Children, awakened by the rat-a-tat-tat, leaned out of the windows to see what the postman had brought. 'Thank you,' they called when they heard what had happened. 'Hope your father is soon well again!'

On to the farm on the brow of the hill. Rat-a-tat-tat. On to the next farm behind the clump of trees. Rat-a-tat-tat. The little grey farm at the foot of the hill was next. Rat-a-tat-tat. The pile of parcels grew a little smaller.

'Ah, a letter from my son, so far away in Sweden,' said one lady. 'I knew my sister wouldn't forget me,' said another as she came to the door.

But all the time the snow fell and the wind grew stronger. And Ola grew more tired. Once Blackie stumbled and a pile of letters fell into the snow. It took many minutes to pick them all up and make sure none were left behind. As they journeyed from farm to farm, village to village, it soon became clear that Blackie would go no further. She was exhausted. It was one of the snowiest Christmas Eves for many years.

Near the end of the journey Ola took letters to his Aunt Hanna and Uncle Mons in their farmhouse deep in the folds of the hills. His rat-a-tat-tat brought them to the door. 'Ola' said Aunt Hanna. 'Where is your father?' Ola told them the story as he sat by their blazing fire and drank some warm soup. 'You must stay here tonight,' Aunt Hanna said. But Ola shook his head. He had promised his father. The people trusted him. The post must get through. There were two parcels and sixteen letters still left.

Blackie was too tired. Ola knew she could go no further. Uncle Mons led the horse to the stable. Ola fitted on the skis his uncle lent him and set out alone. It was getting dark now. The job had taken all day. The sack on his back felt heavy and the rat-a-tat-tat on the doors was not as strong as earlier in the day.

The last parcel was for an old lady they all called Mother Elin. 'From my daughter in Oslo,' she cried. 'I knew she wouldn't forget me. And I knew I could trust the postman – or his big grown-up son – to bring it for me. 'Ola watched as she unpacked a large ham, coffee, nuts, dates, chocolate, and a pudding. 'For you,' she said to Ola, giving him the biggest bar of chocolate in the parcel. Ola set out in the snow again.

Back home the family had watched anxiously all day. There never had been such snow, they thought. And the wind was so strong. Would Ola find his way? Perhaps some of the signposts were broken down. Blackie was only a small horse. Would she tire and fall? 'Dear God,' whispered mother, 'let nothing happen to Ola.' They all waited, father fretfully on his bed. Even Marit could not play with her dolls. She was thinking of Ola in the cold outside.

Suddenly the door opened. A blast of cold air entered the room. It was mother going out, a thick shawl wrapped over her shoulders. They heard her call, 'Ola! Ola!' but there was no reply. Again, 'Ola, Ola!' And again. Again. Then, at last, a happy shout. 'I can see him! There he is! But so slowly he walks in the deep snow.' Then in she came with Ola, a wet, tired, cold, but very happy boy as mother fussed around him to find warm, dry clothes and good food. Ola thought of Blackie snugly asleep in his uncle's stable.

Ola slept sound and long. But into his dreams came the Christmas sound that had made so many people happy that day. Rat-a-tat-tat, rat-a-tat-tat, the postman's Christmas sound.

Christmas music *Play a record/cassette of popular Christmas music. As the music comes to an end a pianist begins to play typical party music and, at a pre-arranged signal, a group of children come forward to play a musical game, e.g. 'Here we go round the mulberry bush' or 'Oranges and lemons'. Invite other children and adults to join in. Pull crackers. Put on any hats that are inside the crackers. Explode party poppers. Play with balloons.*

Prayer

Let us praise God for all we receive at Christmas.

For gifts of many kinds that bring us pleasure;
    for surprises planned to delight us;
    for people whose kindness and thoughtfulness make us glad;
    we thank you, heavenly Father.

For children, with presents kept secret till Christmas morning;
    for parents, giving generously to make their children happy;
    for all exchanging and giving of gifts:
    we thank you heavenly Father.

For your many gifts that bring joy and gladness to our lives;
    for your greatest gift, Jesus Christ your Son, our Lord;

for the example, sacrifice and generosity of his life:
we thank you, heavenly Father.

Teach us, O God, that it is a joy both to give and to receive.
In our giving making us thoughtful and generous; in our
receiving make us glad and grateful.

Hymn See amid the winter's snow

Reading John 1.1-5, 10-14a *Read '... the ... Word ... became ... flesh' very*
*deliberately. At the word **flesh** and without announcement play the*
recording of a baby crying. After a suitable length of recording (15-20 seconds)
continue the reading: John 1.14b, 16-18

Sermon *(about 5 minutes)*
Recall the sounds of Christmas – carol singers, bells, the postman's knock,
the crackers, poppers, pop music, and the angels' song in the shepherds'
story.

And the other sound: the one that comes from the very heart of
Christmas, and without which none of these others would have meaning:
a baby cries and signals that God has visited his people. A truth contained
in five words: **and the Word became flesh.** Flesh like ours to live a life
like ours as the baby grew to be a young boy asking questions in the
temple, a young man challenging others to follow him, a teacher offering
words that have lasted for ever, and a healer who brought comfort to
those ill in body and mind. Flesh, too, that could be bruised and nailed,
and receive a crown of thorns. Flesh of our flesh.

Remind the congregation of the story of the Prince and the Pauper.
A ragged unkempt boy who happened to look like a prince in the country
where he lived changed places with him. The prince wanted to know
what it was like to be 'one of the people.' For several months the ragged
boy knew what it was like to be a prince; the prince dressed as a pauper
knew in his own experience what it was like to be poor.

There was a film which told the story of a man who could not believe
that society still discriminated against Jewish people. So he dropped a
few hints around that he was a Jew himself, though in fact he was not.
Within days he began to receive slights, insults, and prejudice. Only as
he stepped into a Jewish role did he truly know what it was like.

The two stories parallel the Christmas story. God stepped into our
experience. He became one of us. He knows us. It happened that one
day in Bethlehem the world heard the first Christmas sound. *Play again*
the recording of a baby crying.

Hymn Thou didst leave thy throne

Prayer

Thanksgiving and praise to God!
Eternal God, the gates of heaven were raised in Bethlehem.
Jesus left the place of glory to live with men.

We rejoice that he came,
not in military power to subdue us,
nor yet in glory such as would blind our eyes,
nor yet in such majesty as would set him apart from us,
but left the gates of heaven as a child in helplessness,
to be born as we were born,
suckled by a human mother, watched over by a human father,
and so recognised by us.

Raise the gates of our hearts, O God,
break down the stubborn doors of our spirits,
and come and reign among us.

Leader And now the sound of our own Christmas praise –

Hymn O come, all ye faithful

Benediction

A WORD FOR CHRISTMAS

Introduction

One of the dangers of the well-known biblical readings at Christmas is that we are so familiar with them that we can hear them without thinking about their meaning. This service challenges the congregation to listen carefully to the readings so as to be able to summarise their meaning in a series of single words. The service has no sermon; the 'sermon' lies in the reflection of the congregation and the sharing of their ideas. Since each member will hear and reflect in his own way the service is especially appropriate for all-age worship. The leader must take everyone's comments seriously and encourage young members to play a full part.

After each reading, the offered words are written on balloons which will have been blown up during the service. A broad, black felt pen will be found most useful. Towards the end of the service the balloons are tossed about by the congregation, hand to hand, to symbolise 'sharing the word'. They will then be taken home through the streets; the Christmas words are for the world as well as for the Church.

Two 'choirs' are pressed-ganged into service, each having four members. The leader should have a clear idea who is going to ask to 'volunteer'. A ladies' 'choir' will in fact become readers; a male voice 'choir' will be given the task of blowing up the balloons. Three of them will not know this when they are drawn from the congregation; one needs to be taken into the leader's confidence in order to organise the final sharing of the balloons. Choose men with plenty of breath and the world's worst voices! This is a service for a congregation with a sense of fun.

Preparation

Have marked Bibles ready for the readers. Obtain twenty or more balloons, plus one large one; also a broad, black felt marker. Several large plastic bags (dustbin size) will be useful to store the balloons.

The Festival Service

Call to Worship

Go out of the gates, go out,
  prepare a road for my people;
  build a highway, build it up,
  clear away the boulders;
  raise a signal to the peoples.
This is the Lord's proclamation
  to earth's farthest bounds:
Tell the daughter of Zion,
Behold, your deliverance has come.

(Isaiah 62.10-11a, NEB)

Hymn Christians, awake, salute the happy morn

Leader Christmas again! It brings its own special joys – and its dangers, perhaps the greatest of which is our over-familiarity with well-known stories and long-loved carols. Even the youngest in church has heard the Christmas stories before, and most of us have heard them twenty, forty, eighty times or more, year after year. They can stand repetition. They keep fresh, but only if from time to time we consciously search for their inner meaning, and expect to hear new Christmas words within them. This is such a time. Be ready in this service to hear familiar words and sing familiar carols but to search out the meaning behind the words.

Prayer

Father God, your word sounds out loud and clear that all may hear. Through long years you prepared the way. History has been your servant, the nations the agents of your purpose, and now we have our part to play. The word of your truth has been nurtured through the ages so that we in our time might welcome the Christ, the Word made flesh, who constantly comes to his people.

Father, as we hear again the familiar stories which Christmas brings, may we be delighted and disturbed, refreshed and renewed; may old words find new meaning and well-trod paths offer a fresh pilgrimage of grace. May your proclamation to earth's farthest bounds find a lodging place in us, here and now.

Amen

Tell the congregation that the service needs a male voice choir and a women's choir, each of four voices. Select the eight 'volunteers' (see Preparation, page 12) and seat them conspicuously at the front in two separate groups.

Leader   Christmas ought to have its surprises. Here's a poem.

Reader   Good King Wenceslas looked out,
'Snowing,' he said,
And went back to bed.   (Joan Brockelsby)

Leader   And here's another surprise. The ladies' choir is not going to sing. It's a reading choir. And you are a working congregation. As the familiar readings are read by the four ladies the congregation must listen, reflect, and then try to summarise the inner meaning of the reading in a single word. No doubt different people will offer different words. We will note them all.

Bible readings   Luke 1.26-38
Luke 2.8-14

After each reading pause for the congregation to think, and then invite them to offer their words. From the first reading may come such words as 'accept', 'obey,' 'humility'. From the second may come words like 'peace', 'surprise', 'joy'. Note them all.

Leader   It's time for another surprise. The male voice choir isn't going to sing either! It's a 'blowing' choir. *Produce the balloons and pass them to the men to blow up. They will have the period of two hymns to complete the task but obviously will listen to the readings and story, and share the prayers with everyone else.*

Hymn   Hark! the herald angels sing

At the end of the hymn write each of the words that summarised the previous readings on a balloon. Store the balloons away safely. Repeat the words, as you write, for the sake of the congregation.

Bible readings   Matthew 2.1-11
Luke 3.1-4

Again, pause after each reading for the congregation to suggest words that summarise the meaning. This time, as each word is offered, write it immediately on the balloon. Store the balloons. If insufficient balloons have been blown up note the words until more balloons are ready during the next hymn. During the hymn the leader should also blow up the large balloon.

Hymn   Brightest and best of the sons of the morning

Prayer

*Either offer an extempore prayer which uses as many as possible of the words
the congregation has offered or use the following:*

O Lord Jesus Christ,
You were homeless in the moment of your birth:
  look with mercy on the hungry and homeless of our world today.
You were a refugee fleeing from political persecutors:
  look with mercy on all those displaced by war or hounded by
  governments and forces who seek to deny them their freedom.
You were rejected even before you were born and often dismissed
  throughout your life:
  look with mercy on those who feel rejected by society and lack
  friends to give them hospitality and love.
You still suffer with your people:
  look with mercy on us all.

Story

Christmas Reconciliation

This is a true story. It happened about a hundred years ago. It's about
two children and two Austrian villages. It happened one Christmas Eve.

In the village of Gshaid lived a man, his wife and two children. Father
was a shoemaker. Indeed he was **the** shoemaker. People travelled from
miles around for his shoes. For one thing he was the only shoemaker
in the neighbourhood; for another, he was a very good shoemaker.
Everyone came; that is, everyone except the people from the next village,
just over the mountain range, the village called Millsdorf. The two villages
had an ancient feud. No one could remember what had caused it. It was
all a long time ago. But the people of Millsdorf and the people of Gshaid
neither visited each other, nor spoke to each other. No roadway passed
between the two villages, either side of the mountain range, only a rough
little used cart-track.

The feud caused great problems for the family I'm telling you about.
The wife came from Millsdorf, the husband from Gshaid. The people
of Gshaid never really accepted the wife. She was always a foreigner.
If the shoemaker had not made such very good shoes it might have been
very difficult indeed. Our family tried to ignore the feud. Mother and
children would often go across the mountain to see the grandparents,
and now they were old enough, Konrad the boy, aged ten, and Sanna

the girl, aged six, had begun to go by themselves, though Grandma always sent them back well before dark.

It was Christmas Eve! The children prepared to go over the mountain ridge to take gifts, carefully packed in a leather satchel, to their grandparents in Millsdorf. They set off early in the morning. The winter days were short. They passed the bridge and ran across the home meadow. Up the hill and into the forest they went, climbing all the time, higher and higher. As they climbed it grew cooler. They reached the signpost which pointed to both villages. It was right at the top of the ridge, coloured red to stand out against the winter snow, except that it had long since broken. It lay on the ground unrepaired. No one in Millsdorf wanted to know the way to Gshaid, no one in Gshaid the way to Millsdorf.

Then it was downhill all the way. Soon the children ran into the village. Grandma knew they were coming. She waved as soon as she saw them. Within a minute Konrad and Sanna were sitting in the warm kitchen with hot milk and chocolate biscuits.

The day went quickly. Soon it would be dark. The satchel was packed with presents for Mum and Dad, a few sweets and cakes for the journey back, and two mysterious parcels. 'Not to be opened until tomorrow,' said Grandma. The children smiled. Christmas was such a happy time. 'And this,' Grandma continued. It was a metal flask wrapped in flannel. 'Piping hot coffee. It will keep warm till you get home. Drink some of it if you feel cold on top of the ridge.' By the time the day was out they would be glad of that, though they didn't know it yet.

It had begun to snow about an hour before. Light at first, the snow got heavier as they set off, waving goodbye to Grandma and Grandad. It continued to snow as they climbed up the mountain from Millsdorf. It was heavier than they had had for a long time. It quickly covered the branches, the ground and the rough pathway.

They reached the top of the hill. The snow had covered even the signpost. At least it was where they thought the signpost ought to be. Or was the path to the right? Or maybe to the left? It was no longer possible to see the path in the snow. Down the hill they went, the snow reaching almost to their waists. It became a very slow journey. Then, strangely, the path began to rise again. Were they on the path? They saw large rocks in front of them, snow-covered. 'Can't remember those,' muttered Konrad. The snow still fell. Soon it was almost impossible to walk in it. Sanna was tired and weary. She began to cry, Konrad knew they must shelter. 'Over there,' he pointed. He had noticed a little cave in the rocks. It was dry inside but very cold. Sanna was so tired. She lay down to sleep on the hard rocks. 'No, Sanna! We mustn't do that,' Konrad said urgently. 'If we sleep we shall get cold without knowing it. We shall freeze.' His father had told him that. 'We must walk around the cave, jump, clap our hands, and move.' They looked out of the cave for the lights of the village, but saw nothing. They listened for the voices of people coming to find them, but heard nothing. Grandma's coffee was still hot. It helped them. So did her cakes and sweets. But they were hungry, and cold, and very frightened. Hours passed. They would have loved to sleep, but daren't. It was a long time before dawn began to lighten the valley and they knew they must think about stepping out into the deep snow again.

'Look!' said both children at once. They saw a thin column of smoke rising from the village of Gshaid. They knew what it meant. The people of the village always lit a smoky fire if anyone was lost on the mountain. It might guide them home, and it called the people of other villages to come and help in the search.

'And there!' said Konrad. 'A red flag.' 'I can see it,' said Sanna, pointing. But she was pointing in the opposite direction to Konrad. But they were both right. There were two red flags. 'The people of Gshaid have come to find us,' said Konrad. 'And the people of Millsdorf,' said Sanna. The children shouted, waved, and jumped up and down to attract atention. Konrad waved his woollen cap as hard as he could. Both groups of people saw them. Both red flags moved towards them, from the left and the right, from Gshaid and from Millsdorf. They reached the children together.

And what can people do when they meet on the top of a mountain on Christmas Day? 'Happy Christmas!' said the people of Gshaid. 'Happy Christmas!' said the people of Millsdorf in return. 'God be praised that the children are safe,' said the people of both villages together.

It was the end of a dangerous adventure for Konrad and Sanna, an adventure they never forgot. It was the end of a feud for the people of Gshaid and Millsdorf, a feud they no longer remembered. No one could remember how it had started anyway. The villages were re-united. They say that even now on the top of the ridge there is a red signpost, standing tall and erect against the winter snow. It has its own memories of lost children found, and lost friendships rediscovered.

After the story invite the congregation to draw out its meaning in a single word. They may suggest 'reconciliation' or 'friendship' etc. Write the words on balloons.

Bible reading   *(by a different person and introduced by saying that Christmas has its own unique words to offer)*
John 1.1-5, 10-14.
After the reading, write JESUS IS BORN on the large balloon which should be retained by the leader.

Hymn   God rest you merry, gentlemen

During the hymn the male voice choir gathers the balloons together with the exception of the large ballon so that, at the signal from the leader, the balloons can be thrown over the heads of the congregation and held by whoever catches them. Where the church has a gallery this should be done from upstairs.

Prayer
God has given to us his son Jesus; God is with us now and for ever; God has come to us and calls us to be his people, his family on earth. For this gift we celebrate at Christmas, we bring our thanks and praise to God. God, we love you because you have loved us, and you have shown your love in Jesus Christ, whose life we are called to share.

Saying 'May the words of Christmas refresh us throughout the year' the leader throws the large balloon into the air, at which signal the other balloons are thrown across the heads of the congregation. Give enough time for everyone to enjoy the fun, and then suggest that those who happen to have the balloons take them home, through the streets, a symbol that the words of Christmas must go out from the church and into the world.

Hymn   Once there came to earth

Closing words   *Repeat the words used in the call to worship.*

GIFTS FROM THE TREE

Introduction

Only an outline order is given for this service. Its content will be added as the service proceeds. After an initial hymn and prayer, members of the congregation are invited to take a gift from the Christmas tree. Some gifts are wrapped in red paper, some in green, some in brown. The red gifts will contain the number and first line of a carol, the green gifts will indicate readings, and the brown gifts will offer a story to be read. If the task implied by each gift is explained carefully to the congregation, then only those willing to announce a hymn, read a lesson, or read a story will volunteer to take part. Thus the leader may be able to let the entire service proceed on a volunteer basis. In some churches this may be thought too uncertain and readers and story-tellers may be appointed beforehand to accept the opened gifts from the volunteer members of the congregation and then read, or tell the story.

The brown-covered story-gifts may be actual books, the story to be read clearly marked, or stories typed or photocopied from books.

To add another dimension to the service a number of the gifts will contain a card saying TAKE A SWEET. If a volunteer selects one of these from the tree he simply takes a sweet from a plate and the leaders asks for the next volunteer. At the end of the service one large gift will contain a card saying EVERYONE TAKE A SWEET, a signal for sweets to be given to the entire congregation.

If two stories are used, each of about four minutes, the service will last about 45 minutes. It could be used alone when a short service is required, or could be used, for example, in conjunction with receiving toys at a toy service, or could conclude with the Lord's Supper.

The number of readings, hymns and stories can be altered to meet the requirements of time.

Preparation

It is assumed that there will be a large Christmas tree in the church. Prepare small cards, about 8xm × 20cm, bearing the following Bible references; Isaiah 40.1-5; Isaiah 60.1-3; Matthew 1.18-25; Luke 1.26-38; Luke 1.46-55; Luke 2.1-7. Wrap the cards in green paper.

Prepare about six cards giving the first line and hymn-book number of a carol well known to your congregation. Do not include the two hymns already specified in the order of service. Wrap the cards in red paper.

Select three Christmas stories. Either copy out each story or mark it clearly in the book. Wrap the copy or book in brown paper. Suitable stories may be found in **New Stories for Christmas, New Stories for 7-10s, A Yearful of Stories** (all published by NCEC).

Prepare about twelve cards bearing the instruction TAKE A SWEET. Wrap some in red, some in green and some in brown paper.

Prepare one large card bearing the instruction EVERYONE TAKE A SWEET. Wrap it in paper of some colour not yet used. Obtain enough sweets for all the congregation. Distribute them on several plates most of which will be hidden for the majority of the service, only one plate being seen throughout.

Fasten all the gifts on the tree in such a manner that they can be removed easily.

The Festival Service

Hymn O come, all ye faithful

Prayer

Lord Jesus Christ, flesh of our flesh, and knowing our human
circumstances, come and be present in all our living.
Be here in days of peace that we may use such times for
growth and loveliness.
Be here in days of conflict and hurt that, even then, we may
retain our integrity and Christian hope.
Be here in our questionings that we may use doubt and
uncertainty to grow in wisdom and compassion
Be here in our hopes, that hope may be renewed and filled
with realism.
Be here today in our church so that young and old
together may create an act of worship in which you are truly praised,
the life of the church is enriched, and each of us grows in Christian
understanding.

Leader This festival service will grow as we proceed; its message will unfold. Only two hymns have been selected, one of which we have already sung. No readings have been finally decided, and neither have the hymns. We do not even know who is going to take part in the leadership of the service.

The Christmas tree holds the answers. There are gifts wrapped in red paper: they contain the hymns we shall sing. There are gifts in green paper: they contain Bible references that will give us the Christmas story. The gifts in brown paper contain Christmas stories. As we move through our service volunteers will be asked to come and select the appropriate gift and unwrap it. The volunteer will then announce the hymn, or read the Bible or tell the story as directed. (See Introduction on page 19 for alternative method.) Some volunteers will be especially fortunate. Some red gifts do not contain hymns, nor some green gifts readings, nor some brown gifts stories. They contain cards inviting them to take a sweet from the plate. When that happens we shall need another volunteer to continue the service.

Reading *Invite a volunteer to select a green gift, open it, and read the suggested reading.*

Hymn *Invite a volunteer to select a red gift and announce the indicated hymn.*

Reading *Take similar action for the second reading.*

Prayer

Heavenly Father, at this time of Christmas there are so
  many things for which we want to say 'Thank you'.
We are thinking about the presents we hope to receive;
  thank you for all the people who are kind to us.
We are thinking about the special Christmas food;
  thank you for all you give us to sustain our lives:
  daily bread and food for special times.
We are thinking about the gifts we shall give to others;
  thank you for good friends and the chance to share.
We are thinking about families, parties and special treats;
  thank you for parents, brothers and sisters, friends at school and
  at church.
We are thinking about the coming birthday of Jesus;
  thank you for giving him to us to be a friend to all.
All thanks and praise to you, God our Father.
  This is the time we celebrate the gift of Jesus Christ.

Story *Invite a volunteer to select a brown gift and either read the given story, or hand it to an appointed reader.*

Hymn *Take similar action for another hymn.*

Reading *Take similar action for a third reading.*

Hymn *Take similar action for this hymn.*

Story *Take similar action to select and tell this story.*

Prayer

Life is different now, eternal God, since we have known
  Jesus.
He knew the life of a family with its joys and tensions;
  we bring our family life to you with all its relationships.
He knew what it was to work with his hands;
  we offer our daily work to you: its excitement and its monotony.
He knew all human emotions;
  we bring our sorrows and joys, loneliness and companionship,
  our sense of comfort and neglect.
He knew pain and entered the gates of death;
  we bring before you all who suffer and grieve; let Christmas
  speak of the security of your love.
Father, we greet each other at Christmas time in happiness,
  and we greet you, as you have welcomed us.

Sharing *Invite several children to search the tree for the biggest gift they can find. When it is opened, read the inscription, give a plate of sweets to each child, and ask them to distribute them to the congregation.*

Hymn Thou didst leave thy throne.

Benediction

IT MAKES YOU THINK!

Introduction

Christmas is a rich resource for thoughtfulness. Not only does the season itself celebrate the incredible conviction of Christmas that God has entered human experience, but the traditions of Christmas are also thought-provoking. Similarly, despite the commercialisation of the season, there remains a spirit of friendship and generosity which shows the nature of human feelings. This service explores some of the elements within the season that evoke thoughtfulness.

Preparation

Several readers are required, some of whom need to read with sensitivity. Work through the service, list the readings and poems, and select readers accordingly, bearing in mind the age of the authors *(where these are given)*.

Invite an elderly member of the church to talk about earlier Christmases. This should draw out the meaning of Christmas rather than be merely nostalgic. It could be a talk (3-4 minutes), an interview, or a recording of an edited conversation.

Invite a group of three or four people (or families) to research some traditional Christmas customs *(see page 29 for some ideas)*, so as to share their findings with the congregation through statements or conversations.

Ask schoolchildren to suggest a hymn from school which the adults in church do not know.

Prepare characters, with appropriate dress, for a nativity scene. Include Mary and Joseph, three or four shepherds and three wise men.

You will also need a male solo singer (or small group), and recorded music *(e.g. the 2nd Movement of Mozart's Concerto for Flute and Harp)*.

The Festival Service

Hymn   O come, O come, Immanuel

Prayer

We remember at this time, Lord Jesus, how you came to disturb the world, and to turn the lives of men to God. You brought love to those who were unloved; hope to those who had nothing to look forward to; peace to those who were full of anxious daily cares.

But you also brought judgement to those who thought they were good men; to those who were content with their own lives; to those who looked down on other people and were sure that they knew everything about God.

Come into our lives, Lord Jesus, to turn us again to God, to help us to see ourselves as we really are and to take away from us all that is unworthy, so that we may share in your kingdom and know the joy of your presence.

Leader   Christmas makes you think. Thoughts go out to relatives and friends far away. We recall earlier years. We think about friends and plan suitable gifts. Children at school make gifts for their parents; parents think about gifts for their children. The nativity scene can make us think about the meaning of power, and the strength of humility. The angelic chorus will encourage thoughts about peace on earth. Christmas makes you think. Let's look at some parts of our Christmas celebration and, reflecting on them, invite them to make us think.

First, there are words written about two thousand six hundred years ago. They were written to people languishing in exile. They have always made Christians think about the meaning of the coming of Christ.

The past can make us think.

Reading   Isaiah 52.7-10

An older person remembers   *Either as a talk or a conversation invite an older member of the church to reflect on a Christmas long ago. A wartime Christmas might cause the congregation to reflect on how Christmas joy can break through austerity; a childhood Christmas on how Christmas love was shown in a period of poverty.*

Hymn   Of the Father's love begotten *(selected verses) introduced as a hymn that is about 1600 yeas old.*

Leader   There are many links to join the Christmas of the past with that of today. Christmas customs and traditions abound. Some of our members have been studying a few and will share their findings with us. Invite the group to come to the front and share their ideas with each other and the leader in a short conversation. *Use visual aids, e.g. holly, ivy, Christmas cards, where possible.*

Hymn The holly and the ivy *(introduced by saying that we do not know the author of this carol. It is traditional).*

Prayer

Lord Jesus Christ, like a candle in the dark, you are a light to our lives. Like the evergreen leaves that last through the winter, you are a constant in human experience. You garland our lives with your love, and your star shines bright in the sometime darkness of our human lives. No gift we ever received has matched the gift the Father gave us in your coming.
Thanks be to God.

Leader We have long since learned that children and young people can often see things more clearly than adults. So let them make us think about Christmas. Here are two poems written by teenagers. The first strips the stable of its romance. Jesus was born in unhygienic circumstances.

Poem   Birth of a King

Did you see Mary counting the cobwebs
On the stable walls, waiting,
In her fullness, for the time
When she would cry out
Among the straw bales while the
Cattle watched her labour?
That was the birth of a king
That I watch through the glittering
Of a star on my carol sheet.
Did you see the shepherds as they
Stumbled from the snow on the hills
With numb fingers and the filth
Of old sheep under their nails?
Did you see the crown fall
From the head of a king
As he wandered from the warmth
Of his palace into an ice-sodden world
Waiting for summer? There they stand
With their boxes and pout for the Christmas cards.

I wonder how many times they had to
Stop because they had lost the star?

(Kaye Tompkins, 17 years)

Leader The second poem sets our present day affluent Christmas against the reality of the December 25th many will know.

Poem Christmas

Match-stick legs and belly blown
clutching a bowl of charity rice
in a refugee camp
    Far from home.

Tired and poor, chilled to the bone,
grasping the chance of a stable
Jesus is born
    Far from home

Tired from laughter, food and drink
Parcel wrappings litter the floor
Too much on the table
    Is this home?

(Mary Wakelin, 13 years)

Hymn *Teach the congregation the carol which the children have suggested.*

Leader Let's get to the origin of all this thoughtfulness. It's a familiar enough story to us. Can we see it with fresh eyes so that it makes us think again?

Nativity scene *Create the traditional nativity scene as follows*

Reading Luke 2.1-7 *during which Mary and Joseph enter the church and take their places before a manger.*

Pastoral Music *during which three or four shepherds enter preferably from different entrances and, bowing before the manger, take their places.*

Song Wise men came *(see page 31) As a male soloist sings, the wise men enter, one by one, as each verse begins. They present their gifts at the manger. If a larger choir, or the congregation, can be given the words of the final verse they can join in at that point. The nativity scene is retained to the end of the service.*

Leader Now, let's think. Two poems will help us. We will pause briefly after each one to give us time.

Poems   Identity

Conceived out of wedlock,
Born in an outhouse
Laid in a makeshift bed
    of unsterile straw

Let's trim it up a bit,
Make the cows gentle,
Add a sky of soft velvet,
    and bright twinkling stars.

Let's accent the romance.
Forget the reality;
After all it did take place
    a long time ago.

We know such things happen
But this must have been different,
This was the Son of God
    crying and cold.

Deep down I've a feeling
He refused to be different,
That his birth, like his death,
    was as bad as could be.

If it's different
I've made it so,
Heaven, forgive me!
And that's why I'm blind
When I meet him today
    in the addict, the drop-out,
    the homeless, the hungry,
And that's why they often
    don't meet him in me.

(G. Betty Hares)

Thank God

Thank God ...
for empty churches
and bursting shops;
for the soldier's Christmas Eve patrol;
for starvation
and gluttony;
for reckless randy playboys;
for tenements

27

and prisons;
for apartheid-cheapened oranges;
for boring sermons
and trivial TV;
for minds warped by bent schooling;
for drunks
and thugs;
for wreaths made out of holly;
for mucked-up sex
and prudery;
for comfortable affluence;
for ignorance
and selfishness;
for foreigners in foreign lands;
for missiles
and war toys;
for hymns that can't be understood;
for me
and mine.

Thank God for these
else we would soon forget
the world to which Christ came
(and why)
and lose the meaning
in the cosy celebration.

(David J. Harding)

Leader Now the scene itself. Look at it. Jesus is born. What does it make you think? *(Pause)*

Voice reads: *(preferably off-stage, certainly unseen, but loud and clear)* 1 John 1.1-4, *followed by about thirty seconds of quiet organ or piano music.*

Hymn Once there came to earth

Prayer

Go into the world to be God's people.
  Take nothing for granted except his love.
  Offer him nothing less than yourself,
  And, in going, meet him coming towards you.

SOME CHRISTMAS CUSTOMS

Christmas trees

In Roman times trees were brought indoors to celebrate the mid-winter festival of Saturnalia. Celtic Druids also decorated branches of trees with gilt apples. Boniface, an English missionary to Germany, in chopping down an oak tree sacred to pagan worshippers, found a small fir tree at its roots and designated it a Christian symbol because it is evergreen and points to heaven. Martin Luther is reputed to be the first person to decorate a tree. The use of the tree in England was popularised by the German born Albert, husband of Queen Victoria, about 1841.

Christmas cards

The first card was probably designed in 1843 by John Horsley for his friend Sir Henry Cole. In the following year a clergyman in Newcastle had private cards printed. Some suggest, however, that William Egley who later illustrated Dicken's novels, began the tradition.

Mince pies

Mince pies used to be filled with lamb or mutton. They were oval-shaped like the manger bed, the cover being the swaddling clothes. This is one reason why the Puritans looked at them with some suspicion.

The Crib

St Francis is reputed to have been the first person to make a crib after seeing the cave of the nativity in Israel. He created a nativity scene in a cave in his native Italy to bring home to people the reality of the birth of Jesus. Fashion took over and the king of Italy paid famous artists to produce figures. Scenes are now made in every conceivable material – wood, canvas, terracotta, silk, ivory. glass. There is a permanent underwater crib in Amalfi, Italy, and at a recent French exhibition of cribs one was set on a distant planet and showed the wise men alighting by jet.

MILTON MODERN

Pauline Buzzing

Slowly and gently

Wise men came;
Men of fame:
Gifts to bring,
Praise to sing.

1 'Gold,' said one, 'is what I bring,
Gold to honour heaven's King.
   Wise men came;
   Men of fame;
   Gifts to bring.
   Praise to sing.
We will honour heaven's King.

2 'Frankincense is mine to share;
Frankincense, the sign of prayer.'
   Wise men came;
   Men of fame:
   Gifts to bring,
   Praise to sing.
God in Christ has met our prayer.

3 'Myrrh I bring, to show my care;
Myrrh to heal the wounds he'll bear.'
   Wise men came;
   Men of fame:
   Gifts to bring,
   Praise to sing.
Men will make the cross he'll bear.

4 'Joy we'll bring, from all on earth;
Joy to welcome Jesus' birth.'
   We must sing!
   Let bells ring!
   Every voice
   Now rejoice!
Season of our own new birth.

(Donald Hilton)

Acknowledgements

The author and publishers gratefully acknowledge permission to reproduce the following copyright material:

Quotations from *the New English Bible* (Oxford and Cambridge University Presses © 1970) on pages 5 and 13.

Prayers from *Prayers for the Church Community* (NCEC) on pages 9, 11, 15 and 18 (adapted).

Joan Brockelsby:
  Poem from *Step into Joy* (Belton Books) on page 14.

Kaye Tompkins:
  Poem 'Birth of a King' from *Fresh Voices* (© 3M Young Poet Awards Scheme) (NCEC) on page 25.

Mary Wakelin:
  Poem 'Christmas' from *Fresh Voices (NCEC) on page 26*.

G Betty Hares:
  Poem 'Identity', originally published in *Now*, from *A Word in Season* (NCEC) on page 27.

David J Harding:
  Poem 'Thank God' from *A Word in Season* (NCEC) on page 27.

Words and music of 'Wise men came' from *Sing New Songs* (NCEC) on pages 30-31.

Olive Wyon:
  The stories on pages 6 and 15 are adapted from *The World's Christmas* (SCM).

While every effort has been made to secure permission, we may have failed in a few cases to trace or contact the copyright holder. We apologise for any apparent negligence.